AIM Higher!
Reading Comprehension
Level A

Standardized
Assessment:
Strategies for
Success

Level A

Shepherd • Salinger • Castro
Stevenson • Choi

aim higher!®
Great Source Education Group
Wilmington, MA

Staff Credits

Editorial

Diane Perkins Castro
Annie Sun Choi
Sharon S. Salinger
Robert D. Shepherd
Kelsey Stevenson

Production & Design

Paige Larkin
Matthew Pasquerella

Cover

Kaz Ashizawa

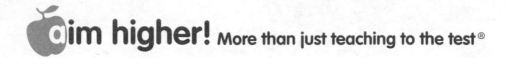

The publisher gratefully acknowledges permission granted by the parents, students, teachers, and administrators of Manchester Memorial Elementary School, in Manchester-by-the-Sea, Massachusetts, to reprint in this book work by Memorial School first-grade students. The publisher wishes, in particular, to thank the principal, Pat Dovi, and master teachers Ruth Goldstein and Maureen Bolognese for their professionalism and dedication to kids.

First Edition

Printed in the United States of America

4 5 6 7 8 9 10   MA   08 07 06 05 04

International Standard Book Number: 1-58171-068-2

CONTENTS

INTRODUCTION

Note to the Teacher: Read this introduction aloud to your students, pausing to explain each paragraph as necessary.

In this book are fun things to read. There are stories about people and animals. There is a poem about a boy with special powers. After you read, you will answer questions about what you read.

In this book, you will learn how to answer questions about what you read. These lessons help you understand better what you are reading. Then you will have more fun when you read.

Four stories in this book were written by kids like you. The kids are in the first grade. They learned how some animals live in the winter. Then they made a book with the help of their teachers. The book tells how animals live when it is cold. The students drew pictures to show how the animals live. Lots of their stories and pictures are in this book.

If you learn to read well, you will enjoy reading more than ever. It is something you can have fun doing for the rest of your life!

Photograph ©1999, EyeWire, Inc.

ANIMALS IN WINTER

by

The First Grade

of

Manchester Memorial Elementary School

Ms. Bolognese's Class	
Darcey B.	Nat H.
Leandra B.	Caroline K.
James B.	Annie P.
Alexander C.	Sam R.
Maggie C.	Ian R.
Samantha C.	Lucie S.
John D.	Jason S.
Maura D.	Paige W.
Grace G.	Lauren Z.
William G.	

Ms. Goldstein's Class	
Emily B.	Melissa M.
Jordan B.	Amy N.
Heather B.	Caitlin P.
Olivia C.	Hayley P.
Alyssa F.	Jessica R.
Connor H.	Kai S.
Madeline H.	Camden S.
Nicholas M.	Carina T.
Patrick M.	Christiana V.
Marco M.	Connor W.

These first-graders wrote the story on the next page. They also wrote the next three stories. They drew the pictures to go with their stories. Many of their pictures are in this book.

Where these kids live, it gets cold in the winter. Plants don't grow. It is hard for animals to find food. It is hard for them to stay warm. These stories tell how animals live in winter when it gets cold.

Carina T.

1

DIRECTIONS

Read this story about how some animals live when it gets cold outside. Then answer questions 1 through 10. The box on page 4 will help you read some of the hard words in the story.

John D.

Deep Sleepers

by The First Grade of Manchester Memorial Elementary School

[Note: This first story talks mostly about hibernation. Hibernation is one way that some animals stay alive in the winter.]

In winter, some animals **hibernate.** They sleep all through the winter in a warm place. Some animals that hibernate are woodchucks and bats.

Some animals are **light sleepers.** They sleep but wake up on warm days to hunt for food.

Some animals are **active** all winter. They hunt for food. They hide. They run from enemies. They change color to be safe.

Some animals **migrate.** They travel to warm places so they can find food.

HIBERNATION

Some animals hibernate. In the fall, they eat and eat and eat. They get fat. Then they go underground to sleep. They sleep through the winter. During hibernation, their hearts hardly beat. They hardly breathe. Their body temperature gets low. They don't eat food. In the spring, they wake up. Then they come out of their underground bedrooms.

Woodchucks

A woodchuck eats clover, dandelions, flowers, corn, crops, beans, buttercups, nuts, insects, and fruit. It eats all these foods before it hibernates for six months.

The woodchuck lives in a burrow. A **burrow** is a home dug under the ground. It has a bedroom, a bathroom, a front door, and a back door.

A woodchuck has sharp teeth for eating. It has small front claws for digging. It has brown fur and a tail. When it hibernates, it curls up in a ball. It sleeps on a bed of hay. The woodchuck has a funny nickname. It is called a *whistle pig*. That is because it whistles when an enemy comes near. Woodchucks are like human beings. Their homes have rooms like ours, and they eat with their hands as we do.

Madeline H.

Bats

In winter, some bats hibernate. They hibernate because in winter it is too hard to find food. They hibernate in caves, old barns, and attics. They hang upside down by their claws, and they curl their wings into their bodies.

Bats are mammals. Bat babies are born alive. They do not come out of eggs. Bat babies drink milk from their mothers.

Bats look for food at night. They eat bugs, mosquitoes, grasshoppers, and beetles. Bats help farmers because they eat insects that hurt crops.

Bats don't see well. They use **echolocation,** or beeping noises, to find food. *Echo* means a sound that bounces back to you.

Alyssa F.

The sound bounces back like a ball bouncing off a wall. *Location* means place. The bats make a beeping sound. They hear the echo when the sound bounces off things. That way they know where things are. 🍎

Words from the Story

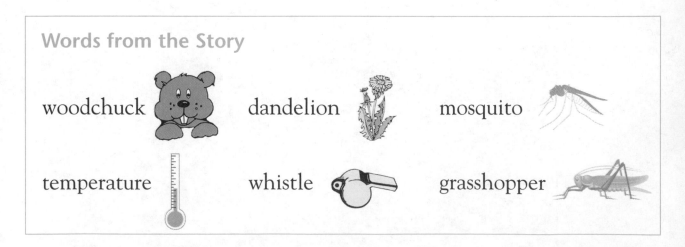

woodchuck

dandelion

mosquito

temperature

whistle

grasshopper

1 What happens while animals hibernate?

   Ⓐ Their hearts beat very fast.

   Ⓑ They hardly breathe.

   Ⓒ They get very hot.

   Ⓓ They eat a lot of food.

2 Some animals hibernate in winter. What does *hibernate* mean?

   Ⓐ fly away to a warm place

   Ⓑ change color to be safe

   Ⓒ sleep all winter in a warm place

   Ⓓ hunt for food

3 Some animals are active all winter. What does *active* mean?

   Ⓐ fat

   Ⓑ lazy

   Ⓒ cold

   Ⓓ busy

Camden S.

4 A woodchuck's home is called

   Ⓐ a burrow.

   Ⓑ a barn.

   Ⓒ a buttercup.

   Ⓓ a bug.

5 How can bats find food at night when it is dark?

(A) They use flashlights.

(B) They have very good eyes.

(C) They use beeping noises to find food.

(D) They eat plants.

6 What is this story mostly about?

(A) birds

(B) bats at night

(C) burrows under the ground

(D) animals that hibernate

7 What do you learn about animals from this story?

(A) All animals hibernate in winter.

(B) Most animals go to the beach in the winter.

(C) Animals have different ways of staying alive through the winter.

(D) It is easy for animals to find food in the winter.

Heather B.

8 What is the LAST thing to happen?

(A) The animal eats and eats and eats.

(B) The animal wakes up.

(C) The animal goes underground to sleep.

(D) The animal's heart slows down.

9 Why are woodchucks called *whistle pigs*?

(A) because woodchucks carry whistles around their necks

(B) because woodchucks whistle when an enemy comes near

(C) because woodchucks come when you whistle to them

(D) because mother woodchucks whistle to call their children

10 How do you think farmers feel about bats?

(A) They like to have bats on their farms.

(B) They are scared of bats.

(C) They like to cook food for bats.

(D) They want the bats to go away.

Leandra B.

LESSON 1   *What Is A Multiple-Choice Question?*

You learn when you read. You can answer questions about what you read. When you answer a question, you find out what you have learned.

One kind of question is a multiple-choice question. *Multiple* means "many." A *choice* is something you can pick. To answer a **multiple-choice question,** you have to pick one answer. Most of the answers are wrong. You have to choose the best answer. The answers have letters as their names.

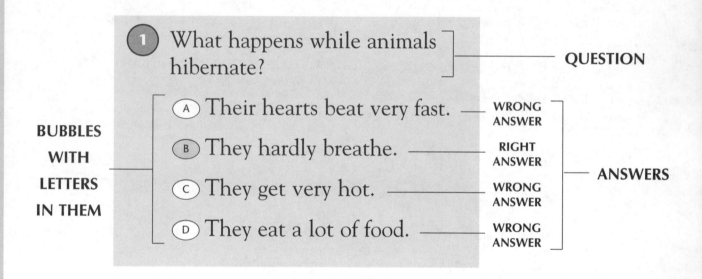

Step by Step

Look at question 1. The question asks you what happens while animals hibernate. You have four answers to pick from. The answers are named A, B, C, and D. Three of the answers are wrong. You have to find the one answer that is right. Then you color in the bubble next to the answer you choose.

Let's look for the answer in the story.

Look at the word HIBERNATION at the top of page 3. This is a **heading.** It tells what this part of the story is about. This part tells you what happens while animals hibernate. It says, "During hibernation, their hearts hardly beat. They hardly breathe. Their body temperature gets low. They don't eat food."

Look at the answers for question 1. Which one tells what happens during hibernation? Answer A says, "Their hearts beat very fast." You know that this answer is wrong because the story says, "Their hearts *hardly* beat."

Answer C says, "They get very hot." The story says, "Their body temperature gets low." *Temperature* means how hot or cold something is. If their temperature is low, they are cold, not hot. Answer C cannot be right.

Answer D says, "They eat a lot of food." The animals eat a lot of food in the fall, *before* they hibernate. The story tells you that *during* hibernation, "They *don't* eat food." Answer D cannot be right.

Now try answer B, "They hardly breathe." The story says that during hibernation, animals "hardly breathe." Answer B is right. The bubble for answer B is colored in for you.

Jason S.

Tips

📖 Read carefully. Look in the story for the answers to questions.

📖 Read the headings in a story. A heading tells you what that part of the story is about.

📖 Always read all the answers. Rule out the ones that are wrong. Only fill in the bubble for the best answer.

Your Turn

This paragraph is from a book about space. Read the heading. Then answer question 1. Then read the paragraph and answer question 2.

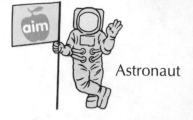

Astronaut

| SPACE FOOD | — heading |

What do astronauts eat in space? Some of their food is just like what you buy in the store. They eat peanut butter, cookies, and fruit in cans. Some of their food is ready to eat. One kind of ready-to-eat meal is spaghetti and meatballs. Some astronaut food is dried before it is taken into space. The water is taken out of the food. When the astronauts are ready to eat, they put water back into the food.

paragraph

1 What will this paragraph be about?

(A) eating in space

(B) sleeping in space

(C) space travel

(D) space animals

2 What is one way that people get food in space?

(A) They grow food in gardens.

(B) They go fishing.

(C) They put water back into dried foods.

(D) They pick fruit from trees.

LESSON 2

How to Answer Questions About What Words Mean

2 Some animals hibernate in winter. What does *hibernate* mean?

Ⓐ fly away to a warm place

Ⓑ change color to be safe

Ⓒ sleep all winter in a warm place

Ⓓ hunt for food

Emily B.

Step by Step

This question asks you what the word *hibernate* means. Let's look for the best answer. Look at the first part of the story. It says, "In winter, some animals **hibernate.** They sleep all through the winter in a warm place." The word **hibernate** is in dark letters. That means the word is new or important. The story tells you what the words in dark letters mean. This story tells you what **hibernate** means. It says, "They sleep all through the winter in a warm place."

Look at the answers. Which answer means the same as *hibernate?* Answer C says "sleep all winter in a warm place." That is like what the story says.

Let's make sure that we have the best answer. Look at the other answers. Do they tell what *hibernate* means? No. Answer C is the best. The bubble for answer C is filled in for you.

3 Some animals are active all winter. What does *active* mean?

A fat

B lazy

C cold

D busy

Connor H.

Step by Step

Here is another question that asks what a word means. Let's look in the story for the word *active*. What does the story say about animals that are active? It says, "Some animals are **active** all winter. They hunt for food. They hide. They run from enemies." It does not say that these animals are fat, so answer A is wrong. The story does not say that the animals are lazy, so answer B is wrong too. They might get cold (answer C), but that is not what the story says.

These animals do not sleep all winter. They are doing many things. The word *busy* (answer D) tells what these animals are like. They are busy all winter. They hunt and hide and run. Answer D is the best answer. The bubble next to answer D is dark.

Tips

When you see a word you do not know, look at the words around it. They might give you hints about what the word means.

Look at words with dark letters. The story might tell you what these words mean.

Your Turn

The Wilson family is going to climb Eagle Mountain on Saturday. Gina is enthusiastic about the hike. She can't wait to go. She likes to be outside. She is looking forward to seeing the view from the top. Gina's brother Gilbert is reluctant to go. He likes being with his family. But he is afraid that hiking will be too hard. He is scared of being up high. He wishes he could stay home.

1 Gina is *enthusiastic* about going hiking. What does this mean?

(A) She wants to go very much.

(B) She doesn't care if she goes or not.

(C) She is very scared about it.

(D) She is too lazy to go.

2 Gilbert is *reluctant* about hiking. What does this mean?

(A) He can't wait to go.

(B) He would rather not go.

(C) He thinks hiking is for babies.

(D) He doesn't care if he goes or not.

See—You can figure out what hard words mean!

LESSON 3 *How to Answer Questions About Details*

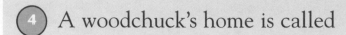

4 A woodchuck's home is called

   A a burrow.

   B a barn.

   C a buttercup.

   D a bug.

Sam R.

Step by Step

Question 5 asks you what a woodchuck's home is called. This is one small fact in the story. One small part of a story is called a **detail.**

Let's look for the answer. Find the heading that says "Woodchucks." Look in that part for the word *home.* If you find the word *home,* you might find the answer to this question. A word that can help you find the answer to a question is called a **key word.**

When you find the key word *home,* read the part around it. The story says, "The woodchuck lives in a burrow. A **burrow** is a home dug under the ground." Now you know that a woodchuck's home is called "a burrow" (answer A). The other answers are words in the story, but none of them is a name for a woodchuck's home.

To answer this question, you have to finish the sentence with the right word. Pick out your answer. Then read the sentence with your word in it. Be sure that your answer makes sense. What if you picked answer D? It would say, "A woodchuck's home is called a bug." Does that make sense? No! That is why answer D is wrong.

5 How can bats find food at night when it is dark?

Ⓐ They use flashlights.

Ⓑ They have very good eyes.

Ⓒ They use beeping noises to find food.

Ⓓ They eat plants.

Maggie C.

Step by Step

Question 5 also asks about a detail in the story. It asks about bats. You will find the answer under the heading that says "Bats."

Pick out a key word from the question. What would be a good key word? You might pick the word *food* or the word *night*. The story says bats look for food at night. It tells how they find food in the dark.

Answer A is a silly answer, so you know that it is wrong. You might think that bats can see at night because their eyes are good (answer B). The story says, "Bats don't see well." It might be easy to find plants to eat (answer D). But the story says bats eat "bugs, mosquitoes, grasshoppers, and beetles," not plants.

Now check answer C. It says just what the story tells you. Bats "use echolocation, or beeping noises, to find food." Answer C is right.

Lucie S.

Questions About Details 15

Tips

📖 Pick out a key word from the question. Find the key word in the story. Read that part of the story to find the answer.

📖 Some questions ask you to finish a sentence. Read the sentence with your answer in it. Be sure that it makes sense.

📖 Get rid of any answers that you know are wrong. Pick your answer from the ones that are left.

Your Turn

One day, Maria went to the pond. She saw seven fish. Six of them had orange stripes. One was white with black spots. She named him "Spot." She liked to watch Spot swim. He did not look like the other fish. Maria thought Spot was great. Maria fed the fish. All the fish swam to the food. One fish tried to eat it all. Spot helped a small striped fish get food. The other five fish didn't help the little fish. But Spot took care of the little fish. Maria was very proud of Spot.

1 How many fish with orange stripes were there?

- (A) one
- (B) two
- (C) six
- (D) seven

2 Spot helped

- (A) the silver fish.
- (B) Maria.
- (C) the small fish.
- (D) the old fish.

LESSON 4 *How to Answer Questions About Main Ideas*

6 What is this story mostly about?

Ⓐ birds

Ⓑ bats at night

Ⓒ burrows under the ground

Ⓓ animals that hibernate

Caroline K.

Step by Step

Questions 4 and 5 asked you about little facts in the story. Question 6 asks you what the whole story is mostly about. It asks about one big idea—the **main idea.** Read the whole story. Look for what the *whole* story is about, not just part of it.

The story does not talk at all about birds. Answer A is not a good answer.

The story does tell something that bats do at night (answer B). But this is one small fact, not what the whole story is about.

Part of the story is about woodchucks. They live in burrows. But the whole story is not about burrows. Answer C does not tell what the story is mostly about.

What about answer D? Answer D says, "animals that hibernate." This story tells what it means to hibernate. It tells what happens when animals hibernate. Then it talks about two animals that hibernate. This story is mostly about hibernation. Answer D is the best answer.

7) What do you learn about animals from this story?

A) All animals hibernate in winter.

B) Most animals go to the beach in the winter.

C) Animals have different ways of staying alive through the winter.

D) It is easy for animals to find food in the winter.

Maura D.

Step by Step

Question 7 is another kind of main idea question. It does not ask about a little detail in the story. It does not ask about just one animal. It asks what lesson you learn from the whole story. It asks what you learn about more than one animal.

Read all the answers. Which ones are *not* true? *Some* animals hibernate, but not *all* animals hibernate. There are animals that do *not* hibernate in winter, so answer A is not true.

This story does not say that most animals go to the beach in winter. Answer B is not right.

What about answer D? The story says that bats hibernate in winter because it is too hard to find food. In some places, plants die and snow covers the ground in winter. It is not easy for animals to find food. Answer D is not a good answer.

The story says some animals hibernate, but other animals use other ways. Some migrate. Some are active all winter. Some sleep but wake up on warm days to hunt for food. This story teaches that "Animals have different ways of staying alive through the winter." Answer C is the best answer.

Tips

📖 Some questions ask what a story is mostly about. Pick the answer that talks about the *whole* story.

📖 Sometimes the title gives you a hint. It can tell what the whole story is about.

📖 An answer might be true. It might tell one little fact from the story. That is not what the whole story is about.

Your Turn

Dan likes to collect things. He learns many facts from his collections. He has more than two hundred baseball cards. They tell how many home runs the players hit. They tell how many times pitchers make strike-outs. Dan also has many shells. Some of the shells 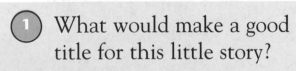 are from beaches on the Atlantic Ocean. Some are from the Pacific Ocean. Now he is collecting quarters. The United States is making a new quarter for each state. Each quarter shows something special about that state. Dan wants to collect all fifty quarters. He wants to learn about every state.

1 What would make a good title for this little story?

- Ⓐ Famous Baseball Players
- Ⓑ Dan's Collections
- Ⓒ Shells From Around the World
- Ⓓ New U.S. Quarters

2 What is the main lesson you learn from this story?

- Ⓐ It is better to collect rocks than shells.
- Ⓑ Baseball players like to break records.
- Ⓒ Coins tell about states.
- Ⓓ A person can learn by collecting things.

LESSON 5 *How to Answer Questions That Ask When Things Happen*

8 What is the LAST thing to happen?

A The animal eats and eats and eats.

B The animal wakes up.

C The animal goes underground to sleep.

D The animal's heart slows down.

Paige W.

Step by Step

Some questions ask you about when things happen. Question 3 tells you four actions. It asks you to choose the one that happens LAST.

Let's look at the part of the story that talks about hibernation. It tells you that animals eat and eat in the fall. Then they go underground to sleep during the winter. While they hibernate, changes happen in their bodies. In the spring, they wake up and come out of their underground bedrooms.

Look at the choices for question 3. Find the one that happens last. First, an animal has to eat a lot of food to get ready for hibernation (answer A). When fall changes to winter, the animal goes underground (answer C). While it sleeps, its heart slows down (answer D). Finally, in the spring, the animal wakes up (answer B). The last of these actions is that the animal wakes up.

Tips

📖 Many stories tell what happens in the right order. They tell first what happens first. They tell last what happens last.

📖 A story may say when things happen. It might say "later" or "in the spring" or "the next day."

Your Turn

My dad likes to make muffins. Sometimes I help him. He calls me "Mr. Chef." We use two bowls. First, I stir the butter, sugar, and eggs. My dad uses the other bowl to mix flour and other things. Then he dumps that into my bowl. We stir it a lot. Next, I get to put in the oatmeal and raisins! Then we put the mix in a muffin pan. My dad puts the pan into the oven. It is very hot. We take the pan out in a while. Warm muffins are yummy! We love to eat them with milk.

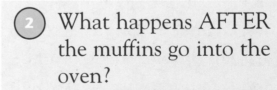

1 What happens FIRST?

Ⓐ They eat muffins.

Ⓑ The butter, sugar, and eggs get stirred.

Ⓒ The oatmeal is added.

Ⓓ The muffins go into the oven.

2 What happens AFTER the muffins go into the oven?

Ⓐ The father and son eat them with milk.

Ⓑ The father and son stir a lot.

Ⓒ The flour gets mixed.

Ⓓ The raisins are added.

LESSON 6 *How to Answer Questions About Cause*

⑨ Why are woodchucks called *whistle pigs?*

Ⓐ because woodchucks carry whistles around their necks

Ⓑ because woodchucks whistle when an enemy comes near

Ⓒ because woodchucks come when you whistle to them

Ⓓ because mother woodchucks whistle to call their children

Step by Step

Question 4 asks why woodchucks have the nickname *whistle pig.* Questions with the word *why* are often about cause. A **cause** is what makes something happen. Running can cause you to get tired. Telling a joke can cause someone to laugh. A good wind can cause a kite to fly high.

What causes people to call woodchucks *whistle pigs?* Answer A is a silly answer. Any of the other answers *might* be true. Look for the *right* answer in the story. The answer to a question about cause often comes after the word *because.* The story says, "The woodchuck has a funny nickname. It is called a *whistle pig.* That is because it whistles when an enemy comes near." The right answer is B.

Your Turn

At recess, the kids all race to the playground. There they can play. They can play games. They can laugh and run around. They can all have fun. Vanessa likes to swing. When she swings, she feels like she is flying. Carlos likes the treehouse. He can see people walking below. Sally likes to play soccer. She has fun kicking the ball. But all three of them are good pals. When it is windy, they play together on the swings. When it is cool, they run on the soccer field. When it is hot, they stay in the treehouse. Friends get to play with each other at recess.

1 Why do the kids race to the playground?

- Ⓐ because someone chases them
- Ⓑ because they can have fun playing
- Ⓒ because their teacher tells them to
- Ⓓ because no one else is there

2 Why does Sally like soccer?

- Ⓐ She thinks the ball is pretty.
- Ⓑ She feels like she is flying.
- Ⓒ She doesn't like to play with others.
- Ⓓ She likes to kick the ball.

LESSON 7 *How to Answer Questions That Ask You to Think Carefully*

10 How do you think farmers feel about bats?

(A) They like to have bats on their farms.

(B) They are scared of bats.

(C) They like to cook food for bats.

(D) They want the bats to go away.

Step by Step

The story does not tell you how farmers feel about bats. You have to think about what bats do. You have to think about what farmers need. Then you have to guess how farmers feel about bats.

Read the story under the heading that says "Bats." You might feel a little afraid of bats. This story does not show that farmers are afraid of them (answer B). Farmers do not cook food for bats (answer C).

One sentence in the story gives you a clue. It says, "Bats help farmers because they eat insects that hurt crops." Bats help farmers. You can guess that farmers do not want to get rid of them (answer D). The best answer is A, "They like to have bats on their farms." Bats help to save farmers' crops from insects. Farmers are glad to have bats around.

Tips

📖 Sometimes a story doesn't just tell you the answer to a question. You have to think carefully. You have to make a good guess.

📖 Look for hints in the story to help you figure out the answer.

Your Turn

I have music class once a week. Sometimes we sing while Mr. Lewis plays the piano. Other times we learn about instruments. Mr. Lewis shows us how to play the recorder. We have to cover holes on it with our fingers. Mr. Lewis also plays the flute and the drums. He says he will show us how to play the drums. Everyone thinks that will be fun. At the end of each class, we get to pick a song to sing or play. We always pick the funny songs. "On Top of Spaghetti" and "I Know an Old Lady Who Swallowed a Fly" are the best. Everyone likes music class.

1 How does the girl feel about music class?

(A) She is worried about it.

(B) She thinks it is fun.

(C) She doesn't like it.

(D) She wishes they could sing fun songs.

2 Who is Mr. Lewis?

(A) the music teacher

(B) a monkey

(C) a man who eats spaghetti

(D) a man who plays basketball

DIRECTIONS

Read this story about animals who wake up in winter. Then answer questions 1 through 10. The box on page 27 will help you read some of the hard words in the story.

Connor W.

Light Sleepers

by The First Grade of Manchester Memorial Elementary School

[Note: In the first story, you read that some animals sleep all winter. Now read about some animals that sleep for part of the winter. Sometimes they wake up to look for food.]

A **light sleeper** wakes up on warm days and eats some food. Some light sleepers are chipmunks, raccoons, bears, and skunks.

Chipmunks

A chipmunk is a light sleeper. The chipmunk sleeps in its burrow. It sleeps on a bed of grass with lots of food under it. The burrow has a bedroom, a bathroom, and tunnels. It runs underground. A chipmunk eats nuts, berries, small frogs, fruits, bugs, flowers, acorns, and seeds. It has pockets in its mouth where it can put lots of food. It has black stripes on its back, a white belly, and stripes on its face.

Raccoons

The raccoon is a light sleeper. Raccoons live in dens. **Dens** can be in hollow trees, old garages, old cars, attics, or barns. The raccoon looks like it's wearing a mask. It has rings around its tail.

Raccoons eat almost anything. They eat turtles, small frogs, nuts, berries, alligator eggs, fish, and bugs. Raccoons eat garbage, too!

Raccoons are **nocturnal.** Nocturnal means they are awake at night. They have good eyes. They can see in the dark.

Bears

Caitlin P.

A bear is a mammal. It has a thick layer of fur. It has sharp claws for protection and climbing. In the fall, bears go into a light sleep. They sleep during the winter. Near the end of winter, the mama bear has cubs. She has two baby cubs at one time. She feeds the babies her milk.

A bear's home is called a **den.** Bears sleep in caves or hollow logs. They live in the forests and mountains. Bears eat honey, worms, fish, strawberries, blueberries, insects, and ants. 🍎

Words from the Story

chipmunk   garage   garbage

raccoon   alligator   strawberries

1 Why do light sleepers wake up on warm winter days?

- (A) They need to eat some food.
- (B) They need to build homes.
- (C) They need to lay their eggs.
- (D) They need to visit their friends.

Hint: Look at the note and the first paragraph.

2 Where can a chipmunk put a lot of food?

- (A) in a backpack
- (B) in a pocket in its fur
- (C) in pockets in its mouth
- (D) in its hands

Hint: Rule out the answer that is silly.

3 What is true about chipmunks?

- (A) They have stripes on their backs and faces.
- (B) They live in the tops of trees.
- (C) They eat fish.
- (D) They move to Florida during the winter.

Hint: Read the part under the heading *Chipmunks*.

4 A chipmunk's burrow has tunnels. What is a *tunnel*?

- (A) an opening under the ground
- (B) a branch on a tree
- (C) a swimming pool
- (D) a kitchen

Hint: Look in the story for the word *tunnel*.

5 Which animal would most likely think turtles are a treat?

- Ⓐ a chipmunk
- Ⓑ a raccoon
- Ⓒ a frog
- Ⓓ a bear

Hint: Look in the story for the word *turtles*.

6 Raccoons are nocturnal. What does it mean to be *nocturnal*?

- Ⓐ It means they eat garbage.
- Ⓑ It means they are awake at night.
- Ⓒ It means they wear masks.
- Ⓓ It means they are light sleepers.

Hint: Look for the word **nocturnal** in **dark letters.**

7 Where do bears live?

- Ⓐ in the ocean
- Ⓑ on the moon
- Ⓒ in forests
- Ⓓ in New York City

Hint: Rule out the answers that are silly.

8 What does a mother bear do FIRST?

- Ⓐ She gives birth to two bear cubs.

- Ⓑ She goes into a light sleep.

- Ⓒ She gives milk to her bear cubs.

- Ⓓ She teaches her bear cubs how to find food.

Hint: Look at the story to find out when mother bears have cubs.

9 What causes bears to stay warm in winter?

- Ⓐ They lay eggs.

- Ⓑ They eat only meat.

- Ⓒ They have sharp claws.

- Ⓓ They have thick fur.

Hint: Read the part that talks about bears.

10 What is this story mostly about?

- Ⓐ very small animals

- Ⓑ animals that live in Africa

- Ⓒ animals that fly

- Ⓓ animals that wake up on warm winter days

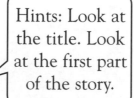

Hints: Look at the title. Look at the first part of the story.

DIRECTIONS

Read this story about animals whose bodies change with the weather. Then answer questions 1 through 10. The box on page 32 will help you read some of the hard words in the story.

Christiana V.

Coldblooded Sleepers

by The First Grade of Manchester Memorial Elementary School

[Note: Here is another story by the first-graders from Massachusetts. Now you will learn about some other animals that sleep in winter.]

Some animals are **coldblooded.** That means their body temperature changes. When the weather is hot, their body temperature goes up. They get hot. When it is cold out, they get cold. In winter, they find a warm place. They hibernate there so they won't freeze. Snakes, turtles, frogs, and toads are coldblooded.

Snakes

Snakes are coldblooded. A snake uses its tongue to smell. A snake has scales on its body to protect it. **Scales** are stiff layers that cover its body. A snake wiggles its body to move. A snake uses its body to feel the ground shaking. When the ground shakes, the snake knows that danger may be near.

A snake eats mice, rats, other snakes, alligator eggs, and other eggs. It has a jaw that can open wide. It swallows its food whole.

A snake can live in a hollow log, in another animal's burrow, or under rocks. Snakes bunch together and hibernate in winter. They do this to keep warm. Some snakes have fangs. **Fangs** are long teeth that can carry poison.

Nicholas M.

Turtles

Turtles are coldblooded. Some turtles are very small. They are only a few inches long. Some are very big. They can weigh hundreds of pounds!

A turtle has a hard shell on its back. It can pull its head and legs inside the shell. Then it is safe from enemies.

In the fall, turtles start to slow down. Then they stop eating. Some dig down into the dirt to hibernate. Some sleep in the mud at the bottom of a pond.

Frogs

Frogs are coldblooded. A frog's eyes are on top of its head so it can see all the way around. Its back feet are webbed for swimming. Its legs are strong for jumping. Many frogs are green so they can hide from enemies. Frogs are amphibians. **Amphibians** can live on land and in water. Frogs hibernate in mud at the bottom of a pond in winter. They eat insects and worms. They catch food with their sticky tongues. Frogs start out as tadpoles. They turn into frogs.

Words from the Story

tongue   tadpole   webbed foot

1 How do snakes move?

    Ⓐ by walking on their feet

    Ⓑ by flying

    Ⓒ by wiggling their bodies

    Ⓓ by rolling along

Marco M.

2 What would happen if a snake sat on a rock in the sun?

    Ⓐ It would grow fur.

    Ⓑ It would cool down.

    Ⓒ It would warm up.

    Ⓓ Its body temperature would stay the same.

3 Why do snakes bunch together in winter?

    Ⓐ to keep warm

    Ⓑ to fight enemies together

    Ⓒ to find food

    Ⓓ because they are scared

Ian R.

4 What keeps a turtle safe from its enemies?

   Ⓐ It gives off a bad smell.

   Ⓑ It climbs into a tall tree.

   Ⓒ It flies away.

   Ⓓ It pulls its head and legs inside its hard shell.

5 What is true about turtles?

   Ⓐ Turtles are warmblooded.

   Ⓑ Some turtles weigh hundreds of pounds.

   Ⓒ The biggest turtles are a few inches long.

   Ⓓ Turtles have feathers.

6 When do turtles start to slow down?

   Ⓐ in the fall

   Ⓑ in the winter

   Ⓒ in the spring

   Ⓓ in the summer

7 What animal's feet are probably most like a frog's feet?

   Ⓐ an elephant

   Ⓑ a deer

   Ⓒ a duck

   Ⓓ a bear

Jordan B.

8 Where do frogs sleep in winter?

  (A) in mud at the bottom of a pond

  (B) in hollow trees

  (C) in caves

  (D) under the sand in a desert

Alex C.

9 What is the name for animals that can live on land and in water?

  (A) tadpole

  (B) coldblooded

  (C) burrow

  (D) amphibian

10 What is true of ALL coldblooded animals?

  (A) They live only in cold places.

  (B) They have hard shells.

  (C) Their feet are webbed.

  (D) Their body temperature changes.

Grace G.

DIRECTIONS

Read this story about animals who stay busy all winter. Then answer questions 1 through 10. The box on page 38 will help you read some of the hard words in the story.

Melissa M.

Active Animals and Migrators

by The First Grade of Manchester Memorial Elementary School

[Note: You have already learned that some animals slow down in the winter. In this story you will learn about animals that are very busy all winter. Some of them stay in cold places. Others move to warmer places.]

ACTIVE ANIMALS

Some animals are active in winter. They may change color to protect themselves. Some grow extra fur. They keep eating all winter. Some store food and eat it. Others have to hunt all winter. Some active animals are deer, foxes, rabbits, wolves, and squirrels.

Deer

Deer have long, narrow bodies. The male deer has **antlers**, or horns. Like horses, they have **hoofs**, or hard coverings on their feet. Their hoofs are shaped like hearts.

Deer live in the woods. They have brown fur in summer. They have gray fur in winter. In summer, their fur blends in with the trees. In winter, their fur matches the color of the snow. That way it is hard for enemies to see them.

In winter they are active. They eat plants, apples, bark, twigs, berries, leaves, and grass. They need to run from enemies quickly. They swallow food whole. Then they run into the woods. They spit the food up, chew it, and swallow it again.

Amy N.

Squirrels

Squirrels are active all winter long. They can't hibernate because they need to eat a lot. They eat fruit, berries, nuts, acorns, seeds, and pine cones. Squirrels bury nuts to eat in winter. They hide the nuts under the ground. Then they mark the spot. That way they know the nuts are theirs.

Squirrels live in trees. They have bushy tails. Their tails help them keep their balance when they run in the trees. They build nests out of sticks, grass, and leaves.

MIGRATION

In winter, some animals **migrate.** They move to warmer places so they can find food. When spring comes, they move back home. Some animals that migrate are reindeer, whales, birds, monarch butterflies, and the Arctic tern. The Arctic tern flies 22,000 miles from the North Pole to the South Pole and back again. 🍎

Samantha C.

Words from the Story

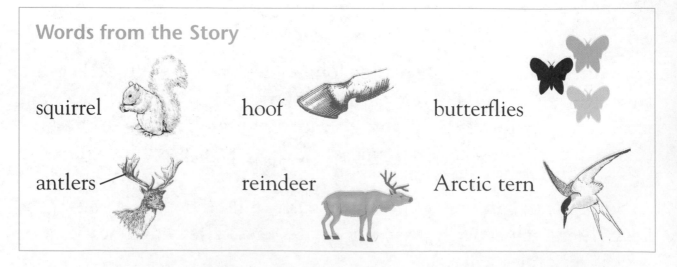

squirrel   hoof   butterflies

antlers   reindeer   Arctic tern

1 What do active animals and migrators do?

   Ⓐ They stop eating in winter.

   Ⓑ They stay busy all winter.

   Ⓒ They lose their fur in winter.

   Ⓓ They sleep all winter.

2 What is one way that active animals stay warm in winter?

   Ⓐ They make fires.

   Ⓑ They grow extra fur.

   Ⓒ They change color.

   Ⓓ They grow antlers.

Nat H.

3 A deer's fur blends in with the trees.
What does it mean that the fur *blends in* with the trees?

   Ⓐ The fur is prettier than the trees.

   Ⓑ The fur matches the color of the trees.

   Ⓒ The fur covers up the trees.

   Ⓓ The fur is softer than the trees.

4 Read the names of things that deer like to eat. Which of these foods do you think a deer would like best?

   Ⓐ bugs

   Ⓑ strawberries

   Ⓒ eggs

   Ⓓ hot dogs

Active Animals and Migrators 39

5 What would happen if a deer saw an enemy?

   (A) It would run away.

   (B) It would climb a tree.

   (C) It would fight against the enemy.

   (D) It would dig a hole in the ground.

6 What helps a squirrel stay in trees?

   (A) its bushy tail

   (B) its big ears

   (C) its little nose

   (D) its sharp teeth

7 Squirrels bury nuts to eat in winter. What does it mean to *bury*?

   (A) to hide in the ground

   (B) to hang from a tree

   (C) to put in a pond

   (D) to bite with the teeth

Patrick M.

8 Some animals migrate. What do they do LAST?

   Ⓐ In the fall, they move to a warmer place.

   Ⓑ They are born.

   Ⓒ When spring comes, they move back to their homes.

   Ⓓ They spend the winter in a warm place.

9 How far does the Arctic tern fly from the North Pole to the South Pole and back?

   Ⓐ 2 miles

   Ⓑ 22,000 miles

   Ⓒ 2 feet

   Ⓓ 22 feet

10 What is a lesson you can learn about animals that migrate?

   Ⓐ Animals migrate to warmer places in winter.

   Ⓑ Animals migrate to colder places in winter.

   Ⓒ Migrating animals sleep all winter.

   Ⓓ When animals migrate, they stay in their new homes for the rest of their lives.

DIRECTIONS

Read this story about how a book was made. Then answer questions 1 through 10.

Darcey B.

How Animals in Winter Was Made

by Annie Sun Choi

The stories you've read so far are from a book. The book is called *Animals in Winter*. The book was written by first-graders. Two classes worked on the book. Ms. Bolognese and Ms. Goldstein were the teachers.

Where the students lived, it gets cold in winter. It snows, and plants die. It is very cold for the animals. Ms. Bolognese and Ms. Goldstein taught the students about how the animals live in winter. They taught about animals like bats, bears, and snakes.

The teachers thought it would be fun for the students to make a book. This is how the book was made:

Ms. Bolognese and Ms. Goldstein taught about bats. They told the first-graders what bats do in winter. They told the classes what bats eat. They showed pictures of bats to the students. The classes got to watch a movie about bats. Then it was time for the class to work on the book.

The teacher asked what the students knew about bats. A boy said, "Bats sleep upside down. They sleep all winter." The teacher wrote it on the chalkboard. Then a girl said, "Some bats like to eat fruit." This sentence went on the board, too.

There were lots of sentences about bats. The teachers helped the classes to put the sentences in order. Then the kids copied the sentences onto some paper. Next, they drew pictures of bats. Then the part of the book about bats was done.

One day someone new came to the class. She was a teacher, but not the kind that teaches kids. She teaches bears! She trains bears to do tricks. She showed pictures of bears doing tricks. The class wrote about bears. They drew pictures of bears.

Each class learned about bats, woodchucks, chipmunks, raccoons, and bears. They learned about snakes, frogs, deer, and squirrels. The teacher wrote sentences on the board about each kind of animal. Then the students copied the sentences onto paper. They drew pictures.

Kai S.

Then Ms. Bolognese and Ms. Goldstein had a treat for their classes. They took them to a sanctuary. A **sanctuary** is a safe place where animals live. It is a pretty forest. There are many trees, plants, and bugs there. The students saw birds. They saw animal footprints, too. They learned all about animals in winter.

Then the teachers decided to have a bear's picnic in the classroom. Each person brought a lunch and a bear. Not a real bear—a teddy bear! They ate lunch with their bears. They talked about how much fun it was to make the book. They looked at each other's drawings in the book.

Everyone is very proud of *Animals in Winter.* 🍎

Hayley P.

1 What is this story mostly about?

    Ⓐ how kids made a book about animals in winter

    Ⓑ first-grade math class

    Ⓒ what bears eat

    Ⓓ kids who go camping

2 Who are Ms. Bolognese and Ms. Goldstein?

    Ⓐ first-grade teachers

    Ⓑ kids in the class

    Ⓒ people who train bears

    Ⓓ people who hibernate

James B.

3 What happens AFTER a student would say a sentence about an animal?

    Ⓐ The teacher would give the student a gift.

    Ⓑ The student would go to sleep.

    Ⓒ The class would play a game.

    Ⓓ The teacher would write the sentence on the chalkboard.

4 The visitor trains bears to do tricks. What does it mean to *train*?

    Ⓐ to hit

    Ⓑ to teach

    Ⓒ to watch

    Ⓓ to laugh at

Annie P.

How *Animals in Winter* Was Made   **45**

5 The kids went to a sanctuary. What is a *sanctuary*?

  Ⓐ a store

  Ⓑ a safe place for animals to live

  Ⓒ a classroom

  Ⓓ a place to teach bears tricks

Jessica R.

6 What did the students see in the sanctuary?

  Ⓐ footprints

  Ⓑ dragons

  Ⓒ books

  Ⓓ elephants

7 What causes a bear to learn tricks?

  Ⓐ A bat teaches a bear how to do tricks.

  Ⓑ The bear reads a book about tricks.

  Ⓒ Ms. Goldstein shows the bear pictures.

  Ⓓ Someone teaches the bear how to do tricks.

Lauren Z.

8 What happened LAST?

    Ⓐ The kids have a bear's picnic.

    Ⓑ The kids go to a sanctuary.

    Ⓒ The kids learn about bats.

    Ⓓ The kids take their books home.

9 What must be true about Ms. Bolognese and Ms. Goldstein?

    Ⓐ They bring deer to class.

    Ⓑ They know a lot about animals.

    Ⓒ They live in a sanctuary.

    Ⓓ They teach bats how to do tricks.

10 What do you think the kids in the class like to do?

    Ⓐ They like to sleep all winter.

    Ⓑ They like to keep bats at home.

    Ⓒ They like to live in the forest.

    Ⓓ They like to learn about animals.

Olivia C.

DIRECTIONS

Read this story about how a sweet little girl learns a lesson. Then answer questions 1 through 10.

Honey and the Bees
by DeLinda Frye

Summer, 2000

Honey likes to go to Grandma and Grandpa's house. The house is in the country. The air smells good. The grass smells good. In the morning, the breakfast smells very good.

Honey and her brother eat the good breakfast. They eat cornbread with butter and honey. Then Tyrone says, "Let's go out!" Honey runs after Tyrone. They leave their shoes in the house.

Tyrone sniffs the air. Honey sniffs the air. It smells like clean grass. The grass is wet on their feet. They run to the swing. It hangs from a tall tree. Tyrone swings first, so Honey walks around the yard.

The flowers are warm in the sun. They are red and pink and white and blue. Honey bends down to smell a fat, pink rose. She hears a sleepy buzz. A fat, furry bee is walking in the flower. Honey backs away. She does not want the bee to sting her.

She looks at a tall blue flower. There is a bee in every blue bell of the flower. Honey gets a funny feeling inside. Her heart thumps loudly. Her skin feels cold. She walks away from the flowers. After a few steps, Honey runs. She bumps right into Grandpa.

"Where are you going so fast?" Grandpa asks.

"I do not like those bees," Honey says, "You should get rid of them. They are ruining the flowers."

"You do not like my bees?" Grandpa asks. "At breakfast, you sure liked their honey."

"Why is it their honey, Grandpa?" Honey asks. "I thought it was your honey. Yours and Grandma's."

"The bees make the honey. Then they let us have some, and they keep some to eat."

"How do the bees make honey, Grandpa?" Honey asks.

"I will show you," Grandpa says.

He picks a tall, orange tiger lily. This flower is like a cup.

"Put your pinkie inside," Grandpa says. Honey pokes her finger into the flower. "Now lick your finger," he says. Honey's finger tastes sweet!

"That sweet juice is **nectar,**" Grandpa says. "Bees drink nectar from flowers. Then they make it into bee food. The bee food is honey. Now, look at your hand."

Honey looks. Her fingers are yellow. Grandpa says, "Inside flowers is a yellow dust. Bees fly into flowers to drink nectar. The yellow dust gets on their furry bodies. The dust is **pollen.** Pollen helps flowers grow. Bees spread the pollen to many flowers. Then they make honey that we put on our bread."

"I have one more question," says Honey. "Why is my name Honey?"

"That is an easy one," Grandpa says. "You are called Honey because you are so sweet."

Fall, 2000

School starts again in August. Honey is a big second-grader now. Her teacher asks the class to write. The teacher says, "Please write about what you learned this summer." Honey, of course, has a lot to say. 🍎

1 What do Honey and her brother put on their cornbread?

   Ⓐ ham and cheese

   Ⓑ peanut butter and jelly

   Ⓒ butter and honey

   Ⓓ ketchup and mustard

2 What part of the story happens FIRST?

   Ⓐ Tyrone starts to swing.

   Ⓑ Honey and Tyrone eat breakfast.

   Ⓒ Honey sees a bee in a flower.

   Ⓓ Grandpa tells how bees make honey.

3 Honey thinks Grandpa should get rid of the bees. What does *get rid of* mean?

   Ⓐ to move somewhere else

   Ⓑ to keep as pets

   Ⓒ to feed

   Ⓓ to swing

4 Why does Honey's pinkie taste sweet?

   Ⓐ because a bee is in the flower

   Ⓑ because she patted the dog

   Ⓒ because Tyrone is on the swing

   Ⓓ because there is nectar on it

5 The pollen makes Honey's fingers yellow. What is *pollen*?

   Ⓐ sweet juice in a flower

   Ⓑ honey that people eat

   Ⓒ yellow dust in a flower

   Ⓓ cornbread

6 Honey is the name of

   Ⓐ a little bear.

   Ⓑ a little girl.

   Ⓒ a little flower.

   Ⓓ a little bee.

7 Honey gets a funny feeling when she sees the bees in the flowers. How do you think Honey is feeling?

   Ⓐ She is tired.

   Ⓑ She is afraid.

   Ⓒ She is sad.

   Ⓓ She is happy.

8 What is another good name for this story?

Ⓐ A Lesson About Bees

Ⓑ How the Bee Got its Name

Ⓒ A Day at the Zoo

Ⓓ A Flower in the Sun

9 What is the main idea in this story?

Ⓐ Cows make honey.

Ⓑ Tyrone gets the swing first.

Ⓒ Breakfast is yummy.

Ⓓ A girl learns where honey comes from.

10 What does Honey's teacher ask the class to write about in the fall?

Ⓐ bees

Ⓑ what they learned during the school year

Ⓒ what they learned during the summer

Ⓓ their grandparents

DIRECTIONS

Read this poem about the magic of writing.
Then answer questions 1 through 10.

Words from the poem:

conjure, 1. To use magic. 2. To imagine
python, A large snake
venom, Poison
Fairie, An imaginary place where fairies live
extraordinaire, Unusual, amazing

Magical Marco
by Robert D. Shepherd

Marco has magical powers.
It's amazing what he can do.
He conjures up people and places
And birds and animals, too.

He created a country, Sri Marco,
Where one little boy had the power
To sit and talk with elephants
For hour after hour,

In the wonderful elephant language
No human has heard before,
About the history of the herd
And fear of the lion's roar.

Once Marco made a red-haired girl
With freckles on her nose
And sent her in a sailing ship
To a land where apples grow

To the size of people's houses
And the worms that live within 'em
Are big as mighty pythons
And filled with awful venom.

He gave the girl such courage,
That she didn't whimper or cry.
She tied up the worms like pretzels
Then baked some apple pies.

No genie from a bottle,
No wizard with his spells,
No godmother from Fairie,
No elves, no Tinkerbell,

Is half as amazing as Marco,
Magician extraordinaire,
Word wizard, first grade, and teller
Of tales beyond compare.

For when he writes in his journal,
It's amazing what he can do.
He can conjure up people and places,
Like heroes and alien zoos.

And the great thing about such magic,
Of course,
Is that you can make it, too. 🍎

1 What does the poem tell you about Marco?

   (A) He is a genie in a bottle.

   (B) He has magical powers.

   (C) He has freckles.

   (D) He is in fifth grade.

2 The little boy in Sri Marco talks with

   (A) pythons.

   (B) aliens.

   (C) worms.

   (D) elephants.

3 What causes elephants to be afraid?

   (A) the lion's roar

   (B) the little boy

   (C) the godmother from Fairie

   (D) the first-grade wizard

4 The girl in the land of big apples has a lot of courage. She doesn't cry when she sees huge worms. What does it mean that she has *courage*?

   (A) She is a chicken.

   (B) She likes to eat worms.

   (C) She is brave.

   (D) She has red hair.

5 The worms in the apples are "big as mighty pythons."
What does *mighty* mean?

Ⓐ tall and skinny

Ⓑ small and weak

Ⓒ red and green

Ⓓ big and strong

6 What does the girl do LAST?

Ⓐ She bakes apple pies.

Ⓑ She goes on a ship.

Ⓒ She finds huge apples with giant worms in them.

Ⓓ She ties up the worms like pretzels.

7 What is the main idea of this poem?

Ⓐ A first-grader makes magic by writing.

Ⓑ A girl ties up worms like pretzels.

Ⓒ A genie comes out of a bottle.

Ⓓ A boy talks with elephants.

8 The poem says that the first-grader "can conjure up people and places." How does he conjure up people and places?

Ⓐ He watches TV shows about people and places.

Ⓑ He writes about people and places.

Ⓒ He plays video games that have people and places.

Ⓓ He looks at people and places through magic glasses.

9 What does the writer of this poem want you to learn?

  Ⓐ that genies and wizards are amazing

  Ⓑ that you can make your own adventures by writing about them

  Ⓒ that elephants can really talk with people

  Ⓓ that writing is boring

10 What might happen if you wrote in a journal every day?

  Ⓐ You would become a mighty python.

  Ⓑ You would do badly in math.

  Ⓒ You would have fun and become a good writer.

  Ⓓ You would be able to make apple pies.

Now go back and read the poem again.
Do you get it now? You can do it!
You can understand poems.
You can understand all kinds of writing.

Happy Adventures in Reading!

Tips for Answering
Reading Test Questions

Here are some helpful tips. These tips will help you to answer questions.

📖 Read the question. Try to think of the right answer by yourself. Then read the answers. See if your answer is one of the choices.

📖 Rule out the answers that you know are wrong. Then look at the answers that are left. Pick the answer that makes the most sense.

📖 Choose the *best* answer to the question. Some answers might be a little right. Look for the answer that is *all* right.

📖 If you do not know the answer to a question, don't worry. Go on to the other questions. Sometimes other questions give you clues. When you are done with the other questions, look at the hard one again.

William G.